You Have a Visitor

YOU HAVE A VISITOR

WILLIAM WOOTTEN

First published in 2016 by
Worple Press
Achill Sound, 2b Dry Hill Road
Tonbridge
Kent TN9 1LX.
www.worplepress.co.uk

Cover image by Elv Moody

Printed by imprintdigital
Upton Pyne, Exeter
www.imprintdigital.net

Typeset by narrator
www.narrator.me.uk
info@narrator.me.uk
033 022 300 39

ISBN: 978-1-905208-33-3

Acknowledgements

Acknowledgements are due to the editors of the following journals, in which a number of these poems first appeared: *Ambit*, *Groundswell*, *New Walk*, *Poetry Review*, *PN Review*, the *Rialto*, the *Spectator*, the *Times Literary Supplement*.

'Figure Among Buildings' was suggested by a painting by John Armstrong and was commissioned for, and first published in, *The Echoing Gallery*.

'The Harvest' was anthologised in *Best British Poetry 2014* (Salt).

'The Colde, Frosty Seson of Decembre' adapts lines 536-537 of *The Franklin's Tale* by Geoffrey Chaucer.

Thanks are due to Stephen Cheeke, Elv Moody, the late Peter Porter, Paul Rutman, Rachel Watson, Hugo Williams, and those at the Cranleigh Gardens and Lamb poetry workshops for encouragement, suggestions and criticism. Thanks are also due to Peter and Amanda Carpenter for editing this volume. A couple of editorial suggestions made by Alan Jenkins before accepting poems for first publication have been retained.

Love to Elisabeth and Lucy Wootten.

In memory of my mother
Barbara Elizabeth Wootten
1934-2003

Contents

Reveille

Day comes up cold,
Though masts over the river
And sails of windmills turning on no grain
All stand-to now in corn-like gold.
Farmhands grab sacks of seed and shiver
To head towards dark ploughland once again.

And here I stand
In blankets at your window,
A last small warmth still leaving last night's hearth,
Your breast, your belly at my hand,
And you, too pretty for a widow,
While men are busy sowing in the earth.

The Ladies' Man

The ladies that he spoke to, soft and sure,
Believed in dresses longing to be made
Of no material but that very shade
Of fabric he laid out. So his demure
Debs' fingers would dip gracefully to azure
Yards of silk, and his housewives' eyes, displayed
A deep vermillion with a silver braid,
Would find themselves seduced by its allure.
On flipping round the CLOSED sign for the day,
Before he slipped his scissors on their hook,
The pleasant-suited draper paused a while
At his tall mirror, practising his smile,
Trying to figure quite how he might look
Now all his many ladies were away.

New Centre

How can you be sad in this wonderful place?
There is music playing and we have cash spare.
Stores are filled with goods we have dreamed of so much,
Back in a city

Where the lives are ruined and sadness will stay
Choking everyone as if there were dust clouds
Haunting us to mess with our lungs and tearducts;
People go walking

Through a world disfigured by time and warfare.
Hurt souls on the thoroughfare grieve for past streets,
Feel ancestors lie down, just under footfalls,
Guilty of living

Where the names of youth have been scored in good stone,
Where old hatred stares from the fresh grafitti,
Far removed from pleasant arcades, these well-kept
Restaurants, cafés,

With their gaming boys and confident pre-teens
Cooing over clothes and enthusing at nonsense,
And the feeling that we are nearly new now,
Clean and undamaged.

O you are the Queen
The Queen of the Inbetween

I have travelled in your country often
And have found your customs strange,
Quite strangely familiar.
I walked around in the unsettled weather
And gave the day to afternoon,
Trusting I'd be with you soon,
For there are things I had to arrange,
Travelling in your country often
Where you know what I mean

For you are the Queen,
The Queen of the Inbetween.

Good Queen, for sure, I know of certain places
Where one notes towards midday
The sharpness of things' edges,
But all your maps are made of faded smudges.
Rumour and a doubt exiled
The failure and the brilliant child,
And your reign has welcomed in the grey,
So those known and certain places
Are nowhere to be seen

For you are the Queen,
The Queen of the Inbetween.

Easter Tide

It is a brisk wind, and the sun and cloud
Head one after the other on the graves,
On cliff-top grasses, beyond onto a view
Of a near sea whose blue is Mary's blue,
Whose boats are being east-blown on their waves,
Their white the white of our dear saviour's shroud.

And further out, our fishermen look up
And figure in the signs of seabirds' flight
Where are the places of the hidden shoals;
They haul their nets like James and John hauled souls,
And bring the living silver into light
Like that upon our raised Communion cup.

Figure Among Buildings

I

Other temples are imaginary.
With walls that figure gods as men and beasts
And ceilings that are painted like the sky.
Here, amidst the absences
Of unruined apses,
Priests
May keep a child as still as statuary
In clear sight of true heavens and not lie.

Traders, for a few small coins, will sell
A scraggy cockerel at the precinct gates.
But wars come and the harvest must not fail.
Men will then trade honestly,
Trusting what is costly
Sates
Gods, so all that's wrong may be made well.
Our chants once more mix with a mourners' wail.

Dandelion Clocks

Ask the horologist, 'who understands
Why watches have faces held in their hands
And calendar girls grow shy when their age
Ends all their dates and then turns the page?'
Then ask the trilobites trapped in their rocks,
'Who knows the time of the dandelion clocks?'

Dandelion clocks that you pick up to hold
Tell you their time was once shaggy and gold,
Wild as a weed and full of fine shine,
Tasting of salad and dandelion wine,
Handsome, they say, as the high hollyhocks –
The time of their lives for the dandelion clocks.

See if the sun feels an ache all the while
He shoulders that shadow around the dial.
See if the grains feel constrained as they pass
The corseted waist of the plump hourglass;
Then beg the pendulum hung in his box
To tell you the time of the dandelion clocks.

Dandelion clocks that you raise to your stare
Say cares and years have so whitened their hair
Or say their children are clung to their head
Waiting to thrive when this dandelion's dead.
See how the children are shaking their locks,
Shaking the time from the dandelion clocks.

Find out if galaxies drifting away
Calculate minutes or know the day;
Find out if molecules falling apart
Cry for a lover that's breaking their heart;
Then ask the tics as they call to the tocs
To find out the time of the dandelion clocks.

Dandelion clocks that you bring to your lips,
This summer's harbours fitting their ships,
Readying rigging for billowing breeze
To send them voyaging over the seas,
Could tell you the time, but how will you know?
Your time is here; take a breath and then blow…

Becoming Trees

You had a bag hung out your window, so you could
  Haul in Italian sausage, cheddar smoked with applewood,
And bread.
And we would lean to eat, there on your college bed,

And sense a student life as richly decadent
As time on daybeds of the satraps of the Orient.
And yet,
  Perhaps we put our clothes on, and we stopped to let

Two travellers with dusty shoes into the room,
Then asked these strangers to sit down and help us to consume
Our meal,
Who blessed us both to know our bodies age, but feel

A sense of metamorphosis that never grieves
  For skin becoming bark, for branches and the growth of leaves.

Coming (or Going) Forth By Day

Day-workers are bussed in from nearby desert towns.
So, while they're here, you get a din of sit-on-mowers
On the lawns, and a drone of the floor-polishers
And vacuum cleaners from indoors. But, mostly, owners
Have little but the sounds of the tick and woosh of sprinklers,
Or birds and insects, to disturb their well-earned rest.

Close friends and family who decide to make the visit
Are helped by understanding guards who all speak English.
Indeed, time spent amidst these safe and tranquil mansions
Reminds them what is absent from the lives outside.
So, as they take the road back east, some long to stay
Where obelisks and neo-classical facades
Reveal their shade along the well-raked ochre drives.

Station Road

The parade seems nice: all the outfitters
And tourist shops have fancy golden letters
Stuck up on their windows. Behind a chain,
Quite near the famous chapel, we can crane
Round the white stones. Beyond, the whole thing yields
To students and to lawns the size of fields,
A river and a punt. Then heading on
Down some occluded passages, we're done.

But later, on the station road, we see
Some dons are pedalling their way so strongly
Their gowns flap up about their heads like wings:
These souls, who leave all humdrum mortal things,
Are flying back to where an ancient porter
Will smile and nod them through the gates; they enter
Where neat quadrangles square the mullioned light
Into eternal sections, all as bright
And sharp as polished compasses; they pass
To dark rooms we may squint at through the glass.

Without Shadow

Year on year, the ground here
Has been slowly raised.
So, when they climbed the wall,
The fall was not that much. A knee was grazed.

But then they made their way
On across my grave
And woke me up. Bereaved,
I grieved for my own death, was left to crave

Fresh life within a skin
Still warm from the sun,
Was made a child apart,
Whose heart and lack of blood forced him to shun

Friends and light. Yet soon night
Pooled beside the yew
And stones. And while they joked
And smoked and drank sweet cider, from them too

My shadow came to grow.
Now, as sunset dies,
They linger, give me hope.
They grope in darkness. It is time to rise.

Advert

Item for sale.
That carefully made expensive thing,
The clockwork nightingale,
Whose tiny cogs and rustless spring
Were polished thirteen times
So it could sing as beautifully
Of human crimes
As one true bird who used to be
In China
In a Forest by the sea.

Discernment longs
For solace in the finely wrought,
The composed unchanging songs
Which are the matter of pure thought,
And which we come to learn
Take the true voice of melody,
And so we spurn
That dull bird's inconsistency
In China
In a forest by the sea.

Please take this thing
For suddenly I find it cold
To hear man's hard devices sing
Eternal verities in gold.
Death sits upon my chest;
I want a bird to sing to me
Of gentle rest
Beneath the graveyard elder tree
In China
In a forest by the sea.

The Remaining

We mourn and, after church, the high lane hedges
Are decked with may, as if for marriages,
While mourners come to linger in the sun
And share a glass or two. Each grandchild carries
Crisps, sausage rolls, or the year's first strawberries,
And talk keeps on the life and pain that's done,
Before it reaches further back, to bring
Siblings and ancestors in, remembering
Odd bits and bobs they had that seemed long gone –
And there they go, the reek of old tobacco
On old clothes, the old voices raised in echo
Of the to and fro of voices going on:
All those remaining relatives now stood,
Asking for more drink, reaching for more food.

Arrival of Another

You knew more about me than I did.
The Storepod docked, the airlock doors slid
Back, and I was naked for you while
You stared at me, till a nervous smile
Signaled you were pleased and you led me
To the Transpiration Room. Here we
Strolled among the trees and shrubs and shared
Our Caring Time. You whispered you'd despaired
Of true love when stationed in a place
Far from population hubs. Your face
Looked unhappy when confiding this.
I inquired if you would like a kiss,
And you nodded, though you did not speak.
So I leant to you and kissed your cheek,
Then knelt down and detached a pale blue
Flower, which I gently gave to you.
I said I was yours, and you agreed
And informed me of your urgent need,
Saying in the Rest Zone we could have
Intimacy with the Antigrav
Turned on. This we did, and you were glad
I outperformed all men that you had had.
Then we stopped and floated while you slept.

When you woke, you looked at me and wept
Tears which floated loose out of your eyes,
Shouting that my love for you was lies,
And reached out to me in our slow spin,
Grabbed at me and pulled my Tender Skin
Off from my arm, showing my desires

Nothing more than programmes, chips and wires.
I tried to explain this wasn't true,
Learning just how I was made for you,
As I too broke down. Now you have gone,
I drift on here, wanting you alone.

Of Late June

Summer comes and is chasing now through evening,
Flashing over our heads and gone so quickly.
Nothing whirls me the way these heightened moments
Dip back down and then dart; they leave us wanting
Grace that climbs up through vertigo to splendour,
So becoming in swifts whose groundless bodies
Hook the sky round the stone of their cathedral.

Just then under the bankside trees I lost you,
Talking softly about your faith and mourning.
Much went past me; your beauty looked so fragile,
Standing here in the maze of thick green shadows.

There are swallows who bob above the river
For the air is so rich with tiny insects
That the fishes are leaping up to catch them.

Fey

I am bored, bored of being beautiful,
Of watching how the blossom falls away,
While always we remain too magical
To keep those ageing ones. Tonight
I found a mirror in the wood and might
Weep at it to the breaking of the day.
How is it we can never make them stay?

Sweet briar roses bloom, and quickly have
Our loveliness; that loveliness will go:
The petals, then the hips fall to their grave
While we go on in beauty down the years;
The mortals touch a dew mixed with our tears.
Our grief will help fresh briar roses grow
Thinking upon fates that we cannot know.

My last would talk to me of how he'd seen
Man's images that move beyond their time,
Enacting far-fetched moments on a screen;
The players all have lost their looks or died.
I could not bear to think how such things lied:
They are immortal but in pantomime;
Their life and art can never truly rhyme.

And now one comes, who strays from human tracks
To ours, into this clearing, where we find
Each other holds the loss each other lacks.
He tastes forever briefly on a kiss;
I feel a little death and sense a bliss
That will not last. Sweet grieving is combined
With dreams till disbelief is left behind.

The Couple

Close after their First Dance,
They looped back through the dining room for grapes,
Plucked glasses from a snow-white table cloth,
So like the drapes of her white dress, and stepped
Out to the terrace where the music dropped
Into the background of a silvery romance
With every surface in the full moon's film,
While her white dress got tumbled in the moonshine
And all their skin was marble to the moon.

They stood near garden statues there,
A hand raising a flute, grapes whose bloom and flesh
In this new light had moonwhite in each part of them,
While she, her hair done in that classic style
With one tress trailed upon a perfect neck,
Made such a sight that tipsy with the white
You'd sway and say of this made pair: 'They are
So like a goddess with her god and they,
Stood here upon the threshold of the night,
Could never change until there came a day
The very stones were broken into dust.'

Carriages

We walked back to the courtyard after dawn.
The roadies were there, packing up the sound
And light, and leads were curling up around
The stage, as the display of ice sculpture,
Which had stood, perfect and spectacular,
An hour or so before, looked on forlorn:
Centaurs dripped and fell, and a swan's neck cracked
To shatter on the stones. Gods, goddesses
Were now obliged to seep into the messes
Of scraps, cigar butts and smashed glasses left
Beneath their plinths. We went and helped to heft
The gear, and saw that all the chairs were stacked,
And then made sure the waste was cleared away
Of revellers who had melted into day.

Elysium

The best time is the summer time,
When cowparsley is high,
And daylight hours of field flowers
Are spread beneath a sky
That drops upon them so much light
And unseals blooms that closed with night.
The best time is the summer time
Till cowparsley is dry.

And there is clover now
And bees to take the yield.
And it is over now
And there are changes in the field.

The best games are the summer games,
The bowler rushing in.
Though voices call and wickets fall
To seamers or the spin,
Men caught in the pavilion's shade
Can play the strokes they never played.
The best games are the summer games
We still have time to win.

And so we find we're staying
After afternoon.
And so we find they're playing
Changes to a tune.

The best songs are the summer songs
With friends and a guitar,
When choruses are all that is,
And we have travelled far,

It seems we've passed all wish to roam
So let the fields become our home.
The best songs are the summer songs
Beneath the evening star.

Hay

Grasses have deepened
And raspberries have happened.
Summer heads into July's
Hot days, where now she tries
To cool off with an ice cream,
Dips feet down in a stream,
Or treads an awning's shade.

Last night the summer laid
Beneath a single sheet,
Till sleepless in late heat
She left her house and walked
To where some friends still talked
In a campfire's shadows,
Then went into the meadows
With July. Dew came down.
Summer's dressing gown
Drenched and her long gaze
Was caught within a maze
Of stars and satellites.

Summer wears two lovebites
On her neck today.
And they are making hay
In last night's field. Grass dries
In the promise of July's
Rich days, so it may enter
High barns for the winter.

You Have a Visitor

And – at last – your visitor has come.
He rolls up casually, as if he were
Merely an old friend come to make a call.
The soft cadence in his voice might be a fall
Of grass which drops back into hay, the whirr
Of blades that take the meadow or the hum

Of the last bus. But he has things to say
And won't be put off lightly. And, of course,
You recognise him now, for he was there
Those other times: he once walked up to share
The sight of blowflies happy in the gorse;
He came round to the hospital that day.

Indeed, now you meet him properly,
You note how much you have in common. Why,
He even went to the same school, enjoyed
Those games you played. Later on, when employed
By the same firm, he always kept an eye
On you, although you were too shy to see.

And here he is in your accomplished house.
As he looks at your possessions, the books
And music you've amassed, the framed photos
Of friends and family on your desk, he knows
That you've loved all of them, and, from his looks,
You know he's loved them too, even your spouse

Has been a soft spot in his heart. Once more,
He asks if you would join him for that drink,
And, once more, you put him off and see him smile,
Quite unoffended. He knows how, in a while,
You'll come with him, may even grow to think
More kindly of his waiting at your door.

Heroics

Kids down the street have been blowing some bubbles which
       glint in the sun as they file past,
Fine as Achaeans in bronze. They are shaping themselves in the
       warm wind,
Foreign amidst all the cars and the walls, with a delicate tense life.
Caught by their colours, the world is transformed for a time,
       then it pricks them,
Letting us gaze at the darkness that grows on the faces that leave us.

Diptych

A Saint's Corpse

A catafalque where the
prayers, chants and movements,
men inward in vestments,
breezed centuries, made skin
dry as any talc.

After Cleansing

In this bed again,
a moisturiser dies inside
your skin, as in
the way dry turf
is freshened after rain.

Portraits

The diaries we wrote
On laptops in the coffee shops of Prague
Are now corrupted files.
That wild sunlit mote
Stands out, although the picture looks quite vague,
A messiness of styles.

Melanie says she will
Still go to Grad School in the coming Fall
Though study broke her heart.
The marble floors instil
A dreadful longing to forget it all.
I cannot look at art.

Nicole's peroxide hair
Drops on her lenses and on gilded frames,
She says she's having fun.
Outside, we sat upon a stair;
The lighters lighting cigarettes made flames
That wept into the sun.

At the Pensione,
We talked of James and laughed about old crushes.
Kate said that she was bored.
And now we spend the day
Amidst these sad and cracking varnishes
Left unclean, unrestored.

Salamander

The sand under the river gathers gold into itself.
Poured from the sun's high crucible, the molten light
Shapes to the hoarded siltings of a floor that is become
Scarcely imaginable save as the flashing realm
Of gilded salamandering. And so the wish to dive,
To swim into a sunken star, to have a life
Turned aureate, amphibious to fire, slinks from the side,
And in the glittered water will credit how it seems
Bank's oaks and apples, soil and flints have all been turned to gold.
It flicks its tail to feel a plunged sun stiffening
Down to the casting sand where all sun's gold is ingotted.

A salamander there prospers without air, gills
Tuned to the sun's own element. It lures a real dive
Which jolts into cold water and kicks on to find
A gold that's unalloyed in grains as tangible as sand's
And winks away through prospects of a diver's hands
Until, air spent, it burns to reach the golden river top.

A Second Meeting

Fervour,
I should have kept for God,
I give to you:
For when you carry water,
You sway
And my eyes go downward,
And when you move in laughter,
I pray,
But my soul turns inward
To dance inside my blood.

Round me,
Men eat sweetmeats and talk.
It seems their lives
Are easy under heaven:
They lie
Like peaceful provinces
That a soul may govern,
Yet I
Know riot from your glances,
Have lain upon your silk.

An Exhibit

When the anthropologists came to our village,
My father would go pick off the plantains
Which covered our vintage Mercedes Benz.
He hoped they'd be impressed:
We too had tradings with the West.

Their faces fell like axes when they saw it.
Upholstery breaks down quickly in this climate;
Even the finest chassis is not immune
To processes of oxidisation.

It was in this way that pride gave way to shame.

Tomb of the Diver

Non-stop partying: drink, music, intimacy,
Young men lounging at poolside, and a momentary
High board diver (beneath him there the surface's
Grey blue sheen) is in midair and unstraightening.

The Sea Girl

I met a girl upon the shore
As I was finding seashells,
And talked to her and talked to her
Of what I was and how things were,
A girl who said how things might be
For one who really loved the sea.

As we lingered there some more,
I told her of the harebells
I found in crowds and crowds and crowds
Where mountains lost their heads in clouds,
Till she smiled and said that she
Could show me gardens in the sea.

Then we both grew quiet there.
A pair of gulls came wheeling,
Out of the blue, out of the blue,
They came to be beside us two,
Walking with us presently,
To mark the sand beside sea.

When they came to disappear,
We knew what we were feeling.
'I'll see you soon, I'll see you soon,'
She said as I climbed up the dune,
While she turned in time from me
Back into the waving sea.

The Wasp Hole

They tack home to the colony, weighed down
With sweetness in the dusk, will come to land,
Drop sail, then walk in from a busy strand
Through alleys of a dark and paper town.
Their fellows have been left behind to drown
In jam traps and must vainly try to stand
On sinking bodies of their fellow damned.
Unable to raise heavy shoes, they clown
Until quite smothered in the red morass.
But these, gone underneath the August grass
Must harbour spoil and venomous desire
Until you pour in petrol which I light,
Consuming wasps, some burning in their flight,
Like Saracens who perish in Greek Fire.

Enclosure

When you left for America,
You collected these dry herbs,
While the local bumblebees
Nosed high stalks of lavender;
Rainwater brushed onto your knees
And your grey eyes filled with suburbs.

And now, your hair smells of the prairie,
And the fierce grey of its storm
Rages in such distant eyes.
Where the grasses are the sea,
Shaping to a wind's small sighs,
You too take the wind's own form.

In the Detail

A good evening to you Doctor!
May I come in? Why thank you!
It is always heartening
When one makes the effort.
You will have the document?
You do? Excellent, excellent!
We have business to conclude.

But first, I have a gift,
Some of that darker wine
I spoke about before.
It needs some years to mature,
To ferment and slowly sift
A summer's bloom and light
Left almost forgotten
In your cellar's coolness.
Such things are worth the wait.

May I take a chair?
There by that roaring fire –
And so early in the year! –
Would be a touch more homely.
You are too kind. And now,
The contract, if you will?

Let's see. You 'this day
Undertake to grant…
And hereby do renounce…
Which will be duly rendered…'
And for this we provide
'The listed "goods" and services,
Including: access to
Privileged information,
Free air transportation,

A personal advisor
And monies on demand…'
Meanwhile you 'retain
The freedom to consult
On futures and on options.'
This presents a problem.
We cannot have you leave us
For the opposition,
So would you strike that out? –
And initial? Splendid.
No use to take such trouble
To repent all later.

Otherwise, this reads
Much as I would wish.
If you could sign down here?
No, that ink I fear
Will not serve in this case.
Just a drop will do.
Carefully… and… yes.

From henceforth my juniors
Will deal with any doubts
You have, but I suggest
It best to live a little.
Travel Europe, spend
The means you have acquired.
Take that Hellenic cruise!
After all, my friend,
What is there now to lose?

On the stipulated date,
The debt must be repaid.
In the meantime, I wish you
All pleasures of the world
And my eternal gratitude
For your endless pains.

The Harvest

One of those rare and yellowed days one gets
In Wittenberg. There's Faustus in his garden,
Its pleasant airs of lingering regrets;
A small wind goes and ruffles up the linden;
From nearby come the pipings of a flute.
This is a place of lost content grown pregnant
With neglect. A great weight of unpicked fruit
Pulls down upon the boughs and the abundant
Roses are tangled by thick ivy vines.

Faustus has changed. His eyes have fed their hunger,
That once clear face has been filled up with lines.
He calls back to the house: 'Refreshments Wagner!'
Wagner comes, quick as Mephistophiles,
To set a picnic down upon the table:
Ham, salted butter and a firm goat's cheese,
A crusty loaf, which Faustus starts to nibble
As Wagner pours a wine of twenty-four
Short years ago. The years have not been wasted
For they have left the vintage to mature,
Be subtle and complex. As it is tasted,
We dwell upon how Faustus's right hand
Has turned to vellum, its veins, marks and blotches,
An occult language we could understand
If we would study hard.
                              The sunlight catches
The swilling of the wine, the earth-red-brown
Of dried-out blood upon the roll of parchment
Which spills out of his robe. On bending down,
Faustus intones old words of strange enrichment,
Then there is darkening; then the heavy beat
Of wings.

We focus on a magpie leaving
The house of Dr Faustus then the street,
Its raddled mob caught in their pitchfork-waving,
The fierce tongs brought redhot from the forge,
As iridescent, flickering, exultant
He cheeks the piebald houses, threads a gorge
Of warm red tiles to lord it unrepentant
Over the Castle Church, before which stands
A monk debating with a Danish student
About debt. And, just as the monk's fierce hands
Are flapping to the heavens, the ascendant
Bird trusts the thermals while his greedy eyes
Are captured by the magic of the market's
Array of meats, the glinting vault of flies,
The pots and bottles, balances and trinkets,
The money that's exchanged for salt or spice
Or grain, the costume of a loud and garish
Huxter who whirls three cups, as, in a trice,
All speculative balls and bets will vanish.
A goat is munching flowers from a barrow.
A stern clerk has been drawing up a bond
For a slim burgher who has come to borrow
Gold. Then the magpie climbs on draughts beyond
That rise among the roofs that keep the huddle
Of poor souls, of the healthy and the sick,
The deathbed, shared bed, single bed or cradle,
Icon and cross, the charm and candlestick,
Until his haughty wings and ours pass over
All Wittenberg.
                    The street becomes a track.
Which leaves to wade its way across the river.
On it a laden cart is trundling back
With what must be the first grapes of the season.
Ahead, an orchard, ladders against trees:
Hands gently put each tender pear or damson

39

Down into baskets, while the windfalls please
The pigs; then long grass and the sleek brown cattle;
The drovers wake a copse; its partridge break.

The magpie's gaze at last begins to settle
Upon long fields of full-eared wheat, to take
Stock of the men and women at late harvest,
The flashes from their sickles, beads of sweat,
And one who sleeps who has chosen to invest
In a large jug of beer. Now, through the wheat,
Another comes to him. Our bird is lost
In want for tiny gleams of rising, falling
Motes from the husk and grain which have been tossed
Up by the labours here; and he is wheeling
In winnowing desires, as our long wait
Is done and ready wings are tucked together
To fall at him as surely as man's fate.
We watch him rapt, then leave the change, a feather
Circling, its quill-tip with a crimson drop,
Then pull back for a crane's view of the crop.

Oranges

Such is the subtle rhyming of oranges
The rhyme of the fruit to the full Seville sun
The way that the planet fashions near-images
Such is the subtle rhyming of oranges
Lovers whose lingerings look to their marriages
Lovers too double to ever seem one
Such is the subtle rhyming of oranges
The rhyme of the fruit to the full Seville sun

Wood from the Trees

Why did you come here?
It is late now and the yellow leaves
Curl into the dark,

And the white bark of the avenue
Receives you; then a house
Where you cannot remember lights,

But panes gone blue for dust,
And still you trust in how an emptiness
Invites you to go stay

Where small claws make a skitter on the stair,
To guess you can make out
The nasty sound of ticking in the wood

And fear the life in lumber,
That timber, which has fallen to the beasts.
Which was granted with the will.

The Apple Tree House

If there were an apple tree,
Here by my window,
Tangling branches
Where red apples grew,
I'd climb to the apple tree,
There by the window,
To see if its branches
Held apples for you,

Held apples for you,
Held apples for you,
To see if its branches
Held apples for you.

If there were a treehouse,
There in the apples,
A lonely thought place
Of packing case wood,
I'd lie in that treehouse,
There where the apples
Could hide a small place
I could be lost for good,

Be lost for good,
Be lost for good,
Hid in that place,
I could be lost for good.

And so would you have me
Climb to my window,
Down from a treehouse that only I knew?
And would you have me
Here through this window
Tell of a treehouses and apples for you?

Apples for you,
Red apples for you,
Tell of a treehouse
And apples for you.

King of the Pippins

Seek No Further, Royal Empire falls
And Pendragon topples
To land on Avalon –
Which is The Isle of Apples.

So, planted there, beneath the morning mists
Whose chills and drips command the abbey orchards
Exists that once and future thing, the King of Pips?

Remember him? Dawn and Earliblaze with Westland?
The Lady Lakeland rose for him;
So came Victories and Splendours and days of Sans Pareil.

Bountiful by Estivale, there were such Galas,
Horses, Summer Champions,
And Jesters, Redsleeves, Franklins, Golden Nobles,
The Princesses hiding Keepsakes and a Maiden's Blush.

Delicious with Ambrosia, the Cox Queen herself,
Quite wonderfully sweet,
Would bend then in July Blush heat.

The nights put forth bold questings for the snail.
Their armour moved on glistening of silver
And blight was still invisible on Beautiful Arcades.

Baldwin, Crispin and the Red Prince fell,
Coeur de Boeuf and Calville Rouge d'Autumn.
Soft rot began and soon most of the Goodland's
Fairest fruit dropped down like heavy Snows
To buzzing enemies.

Russet by Sunset,
Rustycoats and Leathercoats bob on the marsh.
A wounded Monarch rolls to Fallawater
And lays among Blacktwigs and Gillyflowers,
Till many Ladies come to bury him
With Sweet Boughs, Groves,
Where the mist now ripples
Round Avalon –
Which is The Isle of Apples.

Foresters

The language grew, and the Academy
Turned foresters in acres of the word.
Tight thickets and the freshly-introduced
Were all removed, and deadwood and disease
Were treated or cut out. With well-spaced trees
To walk among, it seemed that where there used
To be confusion, shapes of every bird
And every song could be made to agree.

As leaves turned and the trees turned in cold rain,
And the broken wood was all carted away,
Our brushless outings were accompanied
By the north blast which came down from the heath;
A mind could envy creatures lodged beneath
The moss, in a home of roots, or else might read
Within cut bark a sore, bleeding dismay
And long for clearance and the open plain.

The Hazel Tree

The hazel tree upon my mother's grave
Is all grown up. Its gold and silver leaves
Will be the dress my mother never gave,
A dress passed on by one who almost grieves
At how her little girl has passed away
And her young woman's beauty won't return.
I give to her my dress of ruined grey
And all its kitchen ashes, for I burn
To leave the cinder-sweepers.

The birds bring
The softest catkin slippers
And a rustling.

Maple Garlands

They do the sunset hoolas
Decked out in maple garlands
Upon the chilly beaches,
Beyond the breaking waves.

Their songs, the soft hands pounding
On oaken ukuleles,
The leaves, the burning beeches,
The copper of the skies

Make weak men say 'Aloha',
'Aloha' for the dancers,
'Aloha' for the season,
'Aloha' for the sound.

So sailors call from tall ships
And light out for the beaches,
All lost in the strong music,
All lost into the sound,

For love of sunset hoolas
And their goose-pimpled dancers
Forlorn upon the beaches
Beyond the breaking waves.

In Fall

They are the year's top beauties:
Enchanting Fliers,
Their dance and twirl like leaves
Guys so blown away
That no like passing play
That floats up high into the air
And then touches down
Could be so totally unreal
As how after the rain they shake
For guys out on the field.

The touch and tag of summer
Are left way behind
And cheerleaders of autumn
Are crying to the wind.

Pumpkins

Soon we shall hollow out fierce lanterns,
For an October brings with it again
Nights' soothing work of cleaning, oiling guns,
Keen days that grind upon a Hunter's Moon,
Copses, hedges, splashed with haws' stark crimson,
Cheeks of the cock-pheasants that overrun
Lanes and fields pared back to stalks. So men
Take out knives and children will go grin
At the fattened pumpkins that in gardens
Raise up rough and thickened vines: stricken
Nineteenth century divers who are swollen
On their deck and dying with the bends.

Ginny Lee

Striking out one morning,
Cold in the rags of the sun,
I spied Miss Ginny Lee,
But, turning, I saw no one.

And down on Lower Street,
By children playing ball,
I caught her deathless smile
Beyond the churchyard wall.

Sat at the Moon and Six,
Where what I'd seen was heard,
A barmaid leant across
And had a cautious word:

'You say it's been two times now
You've seen Miss Ginny Lee,
I'll tell you son, for nothing,
You'd best not make it three,

That Ginny is a weird one,
She'll win you to her charm,
And use her soft enchanting
To spin you into harm,

For any girl knows lads
Who would take off with her
Get lost or else come back
As half the lads they were.

For what Miss Ginny gives you
You'll always have to pay,
And time you spend on her,
Is time squandered away.'

I laughed and scoffed at that.
I said there could not be
A day I'd be so foolish
As kiss Miss Ginny Lee.

But walking back that evening,
Cold in the rags of the moon,
I heard somebody singing
Some haunting, hurting tune

So lovely that the tears came
Down as I walked along
Knowing that there is an end
To every haunting song.

Then I spied Miss Ginny Lee,
A-sitting on a stile,
She saw and beckoned me
By with her deathless smile.

And Ginny, she stopped singing
And spoke to me in rhymes
And gave six silver kisses
I took six silver times.

And so I stole away
With her for six strong years
And listened every day
To songs that bought me tears.

And now I have come back,
I only long to be
The lad I was before
I met Miss Ginny Lee.

Reformation

Scraps of ceiling,
scoops walked into the stone,
sculptings of a man with toothache

caught matins when the chants were clouds,
accidie in afternoons
and fish
churning in an abbot's pond.

The vaulting,
like the woodland near your home,
lets through the bluster and the rain.

I Give Back His Key

Ladies of the chamber mourn for you
And for a child still-born.
The Prince will take his pleasures
Quietly elsewhere.
And pages go upon small errands
To share your secrets with the court.
I should have thought
I'd not be coming openly again.
The Prince can be as other men,
And I am of the Prince.

Time long since, I came to you
Carrying rare love. The flame
Has all my messages.
The stones have love's old words.
And coded knocks and entrances
Are heard as rumours of the dead.
Your pretty head
I see is now cast down, your hope under a pall.
The Prince requires I meet him in the Hall,
And I am of the Prince.

Piper

In Hamlyn,   the rats drowned in the river,
and we became   a town that had no children:
tops and dolls   over the mantelpiece,
a stopped sound   playing in the streets

forever.

That How You Do

We talk about Sir Charlie,
We speak of Cinderella.
You're up upon my shoulders
With your ladybird umbrella.
We run from falling boulders.
We run from them again,
Then we do the Hokey Cokey in the rain.

We've been among the pirates,
Had cake on seven seas,
Have seen the purple dragon
And handed him his cheese.
We took the fairy wagon
To meet the King of Spain,
Then we did the Hokey Cokey in the rain.

The rain, oh it is nothing
But lots of falling water,
And life can give you nothing
Like dancing with your daughter.
The sun has got his hat off,
He splashes down the lane
While we do the Hokey Cokey in the rain.

Dayshifts

The Man in the Moon will come on Tuesday.
He will wear his grey hat and be travelling alone.
Take his luggage and his staypress suits – and,
Should he speak, converse about the ocean,
Women or the rush on the delivery wards.

I assume he'll take the Penthouse Suite.
Do check the ice-tray in the minibar.
Make sure the curtains have been drawn,
And say I'm sorry that I could not stay –
It's too long since we both worked the night.

Snowbound

At work

sorting candles for the coming dark
fetching firewood

their empty offices
leave fathers

stranded amongst children
to man the last ice stations for a while

A Turn Upon the Ice

Oh, the lake is thickly frozen:
Days ago, some lads with ropes
Tested it most thoroughly;
Even our fat butcher glides
Effortlessly out. And see
How darling Magdalena
Contrives awkwardly to slide
In her oversized galoshes!

It's exciting though, me cosy,
Dressed up in my rabbit trim,
You out cutting such a dash
In the smart new skates you've bought.
Anyone who saw us both
Would observe we're quite the couple;
Anne is wonderfully clever
To have got you to propose.
Perhaps you'd like to go and try
Out that almost virgin ice?

Odd to think of us both skating
Over where we were last summer.
How it all comes flooding back!
Those long Sundays in the boat,
You there at the oars, the blades
Dipping down into the surface,
Anne's hand, my hand trailing downward,
Opening seams up in a mirror
To the sky. Who would have thought
That it would be Anne you chose?
For, after all, there was that time
When Anne slept back in the boat

Look! The spire on the church is
Shrunk no bigger than the needle
Which I pricked my finger with
Doing my embroidery.
And the village too's so small
It appears as if we viewed it now
From beyond protecting glass.
Have you noticed that fine line
Of peculiarly straight smoke
Splitting up a sky that is
An impossibly light hue?
Don't you think that it must be
Rising upwards from the hall?
If we traced it right back down
We would no doubt find your Anne
Beside the kitchen fireside
Lost in thoughts of blissfulness,
Sat down with that seating plan.

Yes, the ice is cracking fast.
We must try to skate more quickly.
No! No! Try to grab on tight.
No, my poor, poor darling, please
Try to get back on the ice!
Don't waste your breath in shouting
They're too far from us to hear.

View

They say the Emperor watched television:
For hours and hours, servants soft-trod carpeting;
No bell, no antique telephone could ring;
Each chiming clock was muffled with a cushion.

Thus undisturbed, he puzzled to divine
Lives fixed in pseudo-documentary
And valued shows whose shaped reality
Could feel to him entirely crystalline:

Contestants were like molecules whose bonds
Arranged them into gorgeous lattices,
And when he saw their tears, his palaces'
Fine jewels seemed cheap by these cut-diamonds.

Still, in the end they wearied him. He rose
In search of more consoling sights
(A footman killed the TV and the lights)
And he went over to gigantic windows

Where snowflake upon snowflake softly fell
Upon his empire's turrets, roofs and squares
And on cold subjects whose uplifting stares
Discerned more shapes than they would ever tell.

'The Colde, Frosty Seson of Decembre'

Now that the sun is much less keen on rising
Than he was, back when he was young and golden,
He peers out, pale and coppery, surprising
Those bitter frosts, sleet, rain and dreary gardens.

But Janus, with two bearded heads, sits down
With wine beside his fire and the smell
Of wild boar being cookèd; and in each town
Each cheery soul you meet calls out 'Noel!'